WILL THE REAL CHURCH OF GOD PLEASE STAND UP?

by
JOHN MASK

WILL THE REAL CHURCH OF GOD PLEASE STAND UP?
ISBN 978-0-9973531-6-7
Copyright © 2018 John Mask

Request for information should be addressed to: Curry Brothers Marketing and Publishing Group
P.O. Box 247 Haymarket, VA 20168

All rights reserved. No part of this publication may be reproduced, stored in a retrieval system, or transmitted in any form or by any means, electronic, mechanical, photocopy, recording, or any other, except for brief quotations in printed reviews, without the prior permission of the publisher.

Cover designed by Gerald Curry

WILL THE REAL CHURCH OF GOD PLEASE STAND UP?

by
JOHN MASK

"Therefore you shall be careful to do as the Lord your God has commanded you; you shall not turn aside to the right hand or to the left."

Deuteronomy 5:32

TABLE OF CONTENTS

Thank You..6

Introduction...7

Chapter 1. You..9

Chapter 2. Your Words...17

Chapter 3. The Church...25

Chapter 4. Pastors, False Prophets, False Teaching.......35

Chapter 5. Traditions..43

Chapter 6. Deceptions..53

Chapter 7. Lifting up the name of Jesus..........................65

Chapter 8. It is Finished.......................................75

Meet the Author..81

Thank You

I would like to thank God for allowing me to write this book, "Will the Real Church of God Please Stand Up?".

My wife, Marie Mask, and children: Marquita Mask, Jasmine Vance, Joshua Mask, James Pettigrew and Ashante' Johnson. My grandchildren: Camari Vance, Fred Garrett and Ja'kira Mask. The spiritual leaders that helped me along the way: Bishop/Prophet Gerald Coleman Sr. (Faith Keepers Ministers, Memphis, Tennessee), Pastor Connie Wright (House of Faith, Somerville, Tennessee), Bishop/Dr. Julian Ricardo Knowles (The Lord's Healing and Deliverance Center, Humboldt, Tennessee.), Pastor James Carney (Christian Faith Tabernacle, Brownsville, Tennessee) also, Joyce Meyers (Everyday Living).

Additionally, my biological family, Darlene Nelson (Mom) who went on to be with the Lord and Floyd Mask (Dad) who proceeded my mom and is resting with the Lord; John Hubbard (Father) who accompanies my parents with the Lord; (Sisters) Phyllis Reid, Regina Mask, Barbara Glenn, Geneva Mask, Stayce Mask, Wendy Outlaw and Sone Redmon; (Brothers) Floyd Mask Jr. and Donald Mask.

A host of nieces and nephews but a special thank you to Alphonso Erving who has supported me more like a brother than my nephew. To spiritual people that pushed me to another level higher.

Charles Hudson and Eunice (Lynn) Foley. I thank God for allowing these spiritual beings to push me, to mature me, and invest the Word highlighted in this book and most of all, in my life.

Introduction

It is time for us who call ourselves the church, to stop talking about the church and start living the church.

If we state that we are about our Father's business, then let's be about our Father's business!

It is time for the real Church of God to stand up and bring the power of deliverance and the name of Jesus back into our homes, and most of all back into the church.

Those that know their God shall do exploits (Daniels 11:32), "As the real Church of God". God wants you to use what He has established in the church.

Exploits means to do more than ordinary. So, God wants the anointing to be used in the church (to break the bonds of the wicked one): to heal the sick, to recover the sight to the blind, to make every crooked path straight (Luke3:5), to deliver His people from the bondage they are in and to set the captives free; To use the power of the people that are looking, expecting a move, the Word and the power of God must come through us.

Just because you're in the church, doesn't mean the church (Word) is in you. I see you might have a question mark with this issue.

The Bible states that the hearers are not justified, it's the doers (James 1;22). So, what's being said? "God is not going to give you anything that you don't want," even your deliverance, yes deliverance.

In this introduction you'll see why the power has left and how we can get back to where God wants us to be.

Are you ready? Are you ready? Well God has been ready for the real church to please stand up! So, let's stand up!
Jesus Bless

"Also I heard the voice of the Lord, saying; "who shall I send, and who will go for us?" Then I said, "Here am I, send me."

Isaiah 6:8

Chapter One
YOU

"Before I formed 'You' in the womb I knew 'You'. Before 'You' were born I set 'You' apart, I appointed 'You' as a prophet to the nations (Jeremiah 1:5).

'You' are 'The' greatest investment that God created. He (God) knew 'You,' and formed 'You' while 'You' were in your mother's womb. That says a lot about God and His character.

He took the time out to know 'You;' To create 'You' in His image before 'You' even knew Him.

While 'You' were in your mother's womb, He formed 'You'. Since He formed 'You,' He knew what He wanted. He knew what He formed in 'You' while 'You' were in your mother's womb. He knew what He created in 'You', He knew what His purpose is, was, and will be for your life. He allowed your father and mother to come together so He could create 'You' and when He created 'You', He didn't make a mistake.

When He made/created 'You'. He made 'You' fearfully and wonderfully made, marvelous are thy works, and that my soul knoweth right well. (Psalm 139: 14)

God didn't get it wrong with your parents and He didn't make a mistake when He made 'You'; male or female, that He created He him (Genesis 5:2). He didn't create/form 'You' to be gay, transgender, bi-sexual, nor did He make a mistake with your sexuality, family, race, height, looks and or your parents.

He created 'You' in the order that He wanted 'You' for His plan and His will to be completed for your life.

Thus saying, 'You' are special in God's sight. One scripture says that you're the apple of His eye (Psalm 17:8).

God also created us to be free moral agents to make our own decisions, able to think for ourselves. Some of the decisions that we make have us to stray away from God's will and His plan for our lives. God realized that and made a plan to redeem you back to Him so that you can inherit the promises that He stated in His Word. 'You' have to allow Him to put 'You' back on the straight path with Him to get 'You' back in the order that He has for you. Then 'You' have to ask Him to save/rescue 'You' from the things that have gotten 'You' off track with His will and Word for your life. So, 'You' have to repent, which means to turn from your wicked ways and don't do them anymore.

Ask Jesus to come in your life to repair the broken relationship; to redeem you back to Him, deliver 'You' from everything that's not like Him and most of all to allow Him to open your understanding of Him (Romans 10:9).

'You' have to reestablish the relationship of really understanding who 'You' really are because 'You' really don't know 'You' and 'You' don't know the true purpose, plan and will that God has for 'You'. Have 'You' ever taken the time out and ask God what His plans are for your life, what's His purpose? What is your will for my life and why did you save me? Most of the time we don't. Also, we don't know God like we think or believe that we do, unless, we are lined up with His word.

Most of the time we rely on others to point us to the plan our destiny, purpose and most of all the plan. God didn't direct that person to do something and 'You' rely on his word more than 'You' do what God said in His word, not only are you making that person your God but, 'You' are in error and God is not pleased with it.

Not only can that be dangerous but it can be costly. Yes, costly. If someone says to 'You' that God informed them of this, that, or the other and 'You' listen to them but its not lined up with His Word, not only are 'You' in error, but you both are in error. Just because something sounds or feels good to your flesh, but if God didn't say it through His word, then it too is in error.

I have a question for 'You'. Do 'You' really want the promises of God? If 'You' state yes, then like God told the prophet, eat the whole scroll (Ezekiel 3;3). Also, 'You' have to be lined up on line, and precept upon precept (Isaiah 28:10). That means the Word has to be in 'You' and 'You' in the Word (John 15:7). 'You' can't expect the fullness of God when 'You' are only giving Him a part of 'You'.

God wants the fullness of 'You' if 'You' expect to get the fullness of Him. Do me a favor, go to any job and expect full-time pay but you're only giving them part-time hours.

Didn't the Bible say, to be friends with the world that you're an enemy to the cross (James 4:4)? "Ye adulterers and adultereses, know ye not that the friendship of the world is enmity with God? Whosoever therefore will be a friend of the world is the enemy of God."

We learn in Rev. 3:20, "Behold, I stand at the door, and knock, if any man hear my voice, and open the door, I will come in to him, and will sup with him, and he with me." That means every day, every time you're breathing His air, He is ministering to 'You' about coming to Him.

When He allows troubles to come, He is telling 'You' to come to Him. When death comes at your door God is still ministering to 'You'.

He is constantly standing at the door of your heart knocking and waiting for 'You' to open up and open it so He can come in, heal and deliver you by setting you free. The only thing about that is, 'You' have to open the door. God is not going to force His Word and His will upon 'You'. Nor will He make "You" study his Word or make 'You' read His Word. Nor is He going to make 'You' go to church or have a relationship with Him. But when your day of adversity comes, when 'You' mocked God, yes God is going to mock 'You' (Proverbs 1:26).

So, God wants you to know about Him. He is a God of wrath, a God of love, but most of all He is a God of order. If 'You' are out of order with God through His word, how in the world are you going to expect Him to answer 'You?'

To many times we say that God understands. That's one of the biggest lies that the devil brought into our ears. The only thing that God understands is what He has given 'You' and that's His Word, and it became flesh and dwell among us (John 1:14).

So, 'You' think they can overlook Jesus, and go straight to God? That's not going to happen. So, 'You' think 'You' can do what 'You' want to do and then go to God praying and think He's going to answer? True, there is a scripture that says the day that 'You' call upon Him, He will answer. True, God is going to answer but He will deal with 'You' as well. God will always send warnings before destruction (Hebrews 2:1) because of His goodness, and His mercies will warn us. He will tell 'You', or inform 'You' if 'You' listen. Things are coming your way. But 'You' have to take heed of His voice and what He's saying. We used to say that something told us not to do this, or not to do that, or go over here or over there. That something is named Jesus, and if 'You' take heed, then He will reward 'You' (Hebrews 11:6).

Now, 'You' have a lot of things to consider: the promises of God, or the destruction and mayhem of the world? 'You' have some decisions that 'You' have to make, do 'You' want to continue in sin and not receive the promises of God? Do 'You' want to continue to stunt your growth with God because 'You' want to do what 'You' want to do, instead of listening and obeying the Words of the Lord? Do 'You' know that disobedience to the word of God is a spirit of witchcraft (1 Samuel 15:23)? Do 'You' really want to hinder the blessing that God has for 'You'? 'You' don't want anyone to tell 'You' what thus sys the Lord? Do 'You' really want God to shut up heaven because He has asked 'You' to change your way? Last but not least, do you want to wake up and find yourself dead in front of God and he tells 'You' to depart from Him because 'You' worked iniquity (Matthews 7:23)? Because in case 'You' didn't know, everything that 'You' do in the body, whether it be good or bad, 'You' are going to be judged and held accountable (2 Corinthians 5:10). Now, 'You' have a lot to be held accountable for and 'You' also have the responsibility.

Do 'You' really want to hinder the blessing that God has for 'You', because 'You' don't want anyone to tell 'You' what thus says the Lord? Just think, no matter how much 'You' read, study and quote scriptures; if 'You' haven't committed to Christ you're still in error or trouble (John 5:39).

No matter how close 'You' are to your pastor, bishop, etc., they can't get 'You' into heaven. No matter how good 'You' think your goodness is, this will not get into heaven. No matter what 'You' do, as far as charitable deeds, your deeds will not get 'You' into heaven. There are no excuses and no amount of money 'You' can pay as tithes, or offerings that can get 'You' into heaven. So, once again 'You' have a choice to make. The promises are yea and amen, the promises. If 'You' allow the Holy Spirit to transform 'You' from the flesh to the works of the Spirit, which are love, joy, peace, long-suffering, kindness, goodness, faithfulness, gentleness, self-control, against there is no law (Galatians 5:22- 23). That's one of the promises, to give 'You' the fruits of the spirit and deliver you from the works of the flesh which are adultery, fornication, uncleanness, licentiousness, idolatry, sorcery, hatred, contentions, jealousies, outburst of wrath, selfish ambitions, dissensions, heresies, envy, murder's, drunkenness and revelries (Galatians 5:19-21).

Those who practice these things are not fit for the Masters use and will not inherit the kingdom of God. There are more promises of God. In Joshua 1:3, God says, "Every place that the sole of your good shall tread upon, that I given unto you, as I said unto Moses." In Proverbs 3:24, He refers to us as "sweet sleep, and in Proverbs 19:21 that He will give us peace from a troubled mind, and in

3 John 1:2, that He will prosper and give us health, even as your soul prospers. The greatest promise is eternal. Can 'You' image God telling 'You', well done my good and faithful servant (Matthews 25:23).

I'm not trying to make 'You' do anything that 'You' don't want to do but if 'YOU' are saved and not living according to His Word, then I ask 'You' to submit or build a relationship with God. If 'YOU' are not saved then get to know Him because every knee is going to bow and every tongue will confuse that He is Lord.

So, why would 'YOU' want to wait until then and are made to say it, while 'YOU' still have an opportunity to know Him, bless Him, received the blessing/ promises and the fullness of CHRIST 'NOW'.

"Be ye therefore perfect, even as your Father which is in heaven is perfect."

Matthew 5:48

Chapter Two
"Your Words"

"Let your words" speak for you not against you" (John J. Mask)

Have your words ever had you tell a lie on someone or something? Or better yet, have your words gotten you in a fight, an argument or even caused harm to someone else? Have your words caused you to leave, loose a job, a husband, a wife, friends, relationships, or kicked out of a club, a bar or a well-organized establishment? Have your words gotten to the point where people rather see you leaving instead of coming? When people see your number on their phone, and because of your words, do they think, I'm not answering it because they are always filled with drama?

Sometimes the words that proceed out of your mouth can be more devastating than your presence. We have all heard the quote, "Sticks and stones may break my bones but, your words will never hurt me". That was one of the biggest lies that the devil will have you believe. Your words have power. Yes, power. The Bible states that life and death are in power of the tongue (Proverbs 18:21). So regardless, whatever an individual says, your words are one of your life's blood. You can speak life into a situation through your words or you can condemn that same situation by just speaking to it, through it, or over it. That we read have meaning and, or power. We were just informed, these are just words. We were taught that what we read and what we speak is no more than that. Do you know or realized that God created words to be positive, to manifest hope, to create life, to create a positive change?

Also every word that you speak, is contrary to the Word of God to bring darkness instead of life; to tear down instead of building up, negative instead of being positive, to bring harm instead of help, you must to give account to it (Matthews 12:26).

We as a people were never informed that our words, or the words but our words, your words, the words that you speak, are spiritual and they bring life (John 6:63). When you release words from your mouth into the atmosphere, your words can carry a spirit and enters the spiritual realm. Whatever your words proclaim from your mouth, to the atmosphere goes into the spiritual reign. Then it goes out to perform what your mouth has spoken. Perfect example, when someone says an inappropriate word to you (cuss at you) and you hear what they have said, how does that make you feel? Do the words prick your heart? Do you react in the same manner that the words were spoken to you? Do, you take to heart or do you just walk away? Whatever method you choose to do, know those words that were spoken still rest with you? If it didn't rest with or on you, you wouldn't tell other people what he or she said.

So, that's evidence that your words have power and yes, they are life as well.

Do you know that your words have power to form life, to bring life, to heal, to speak into existence those things that are not as though they were (Romans 4:17)? Let's look at how God formed life. Look at the creation words that God spoke in Genesis 1:1, "In the beginning God created the heavens and the Earth". So, before God created, He had to think about what His words were going to speak/create and He spoke it unto creation.

God knew that what He spoke through His Word was going to come to pass because He had confidence in not just Himself, but also in His words.

Now, let's look how the Word brought back life, not only did God do it in Genesis, God informed Ezekiel to prophesies to some dry bones in the name of the Lord. Not only did the bones start transforming to what was spoken by Ezekiel, but also the wind. Ezekiel spoke to the winds and the winds obeyed him (Ezekiel 37:1-14). Everything that God spoke was positive, creative and most of all useful for His creation and His purpose. He created the stars, moon, the animals and the birds. Everything that God created was good and very good.

The second greatest thing that God created was man. God said, "Let us create man in our image, in our own likeness." So they spoke men into existence [Verse 26] and man became a living human being.

To heal, He (Jesus) sent His word to heal them and delivered them from their destructions (Psalms 107:21).

Is any sick among you? Let him call for the Elders of the church; and let them pray (speak) over him, and the prayer of faith shall save the sick and the Lord shall raise him up (James 5:14).

Also, your words can speak into the elements and command them in Jesus' name to do whatever you tell them to do. We all read where Jesus walked on water. He commanded the wind to behave and the elements to do something that they were not designed to do: A liquid form (water) to hold up a human flesh and allowed it to transform one area to another (to walk). Not only did He do that, He commanded Peter to do it as well.

You might be saying, well that was Jesus, but didn't Jesus say that greater works that we will do because He went to our Father (John 14:12)?

Not only that, Elisha spoke into three elements. He spoke to the metal of the axle, the wood on the handle that held the axle, last but not least, he spoke to the water and they obeyed him (2 Kings 6:1-7). Three different elements but the same results. Elisha spoke, the elements aligned and reacted to what his mouth commanded. He did that because a man borrowed an axle and it broke and went into the water. That's why the devil wants the Saints and church people to get caught up on saying things that are not in line with God's promises or His plans for their lives. So, your words will not line up with God, and you will not get the promises that God has for you through His word.

Jesus also gave us a commandment. He informed us to speak to our mountains and they shall be moved (Mark 11: 23). So, He (Jesus) gave you power through your words to basically handle your own situation through His Word. My question is, why aren't you using it or doing it?

God is the God of the impossible. Scientist try to understand the plan of God: saying one thing, but my God says another. You can do all things through Christ who strengthens you. The reason we don't see the manifestation of our words in our churches, or in our lives is because we don't ask (God). We don't study (The Word) and don't have the faith (in Jesus). True, we talk it, say it and even teach it but when it comes time to perform what your words say, we have the tendency to doubt, and disbelief sets in. Sayings such as, "I should have been dead sleeping in my grave," or "I could have been this," or "I could have been that," highlights the promises God has for you.

The Word states that God has a plan for your life. These plans are plans of prosperity. Do you know that God covered you with His blood so you could have, wouldn't have, and He allow the death angle to pass by? You may have said, "I wish I was never born," because of the trials and tribulations that came into your life. The Bible says to consider it joy when you face trials and tribulations because it's the testing of your faith (James 1:2-4). Stop allowing the world's words dictate to you what God has preordained for your life.

I have a question for you. Has God ever tried you with His Words, as compared to your words? Have you ever read something in the bible or heard your pastor make a statement, and you say to yourself, "I believe it and immediately God informed you to do it?" For example, when people come to you, telling you how hard times are and they can hardly make it, do you agree with them as the world would? Or do the words you read, or things you've heard that are within you come to change your situation? Did you speak life or death, did you quote you, or the Word of God? My God shall supply all my needs according to His riches in glory by Christ Jesus, [Philippians 4:19] [Psalms 37: 25] do you pray and use your words to bless them? When you hear that someone is dying, do you have a pity party with them by being sympathetic? Do you use your words to speak life into their situation (Psalms 118:17)? When you hear that someone needs counseling or deliverance, do you send them to a counselor, or talk about themes; tell them that Jesus is a wonderful counselor, and Prince of Peace (Isaiah 9:6)?

What are you speaking on today? What are your words creating? What are your words forming out of your heart (Luke 6:45)? Your words were meant to have power and demonstrations. That means faith and prosperity. So, God is waiting on you and your words to change lives, to change homes, to change the atmosphere and most of all to change you.

I said earlier that man was the second greatest thing that God created, the first was His Word. In the beginning was the Word and the Word was with God, and the Word was God. He was in the beginning with God. All things were made through Him and without Him, nothing that was made would have been made. Inside Him was life, and the life was the light of men.

The light shines in the darkness, and the darkness did not comprehend it. There was a man sent from God whose name was John. This man came for a witness, to bear witness of the Light that all through him might believe. He was not that Light but was sent to bear witness of that Light: the true Light which gives light to every man who comes into the world. He was in the world, the world was made through Him, and the world did not know Him.

He came to His own, and His own did not receive Him. But to those whom did receive Him, He gave the right to become children of God. Even to those who believe in His name: those who were born not of blood, nor of the will of the flesh, nor of the will of man, but of God. And the Word became flesh and dwelt among us and we beheld His glory, the glory as of the only begotten of the Father, full of grace and truth. (John1:1-14)

The words, your words point to yourself and you have work to do as the body of Christ. People that want change, must speak it. We have a job to do in Jesus' mighty name. "Let your words speak for you not against you."

"So Joshua conquered all the land: the mountain country and the South and the lowland and the wilderness slopes, and all their kings; he left none remaining, but utterly destroyed all that breathed, as the Lord God of Israel had commanded."

Joshua 10:40

Chapter Three
THE CHURCH

For the time has come that judgment must begin in the house of God and if it first begins with us, what shall the end be of them that obey not the gospel (1 Peter 4:17)?

God is judging us on how we conduct His business concerning "The Church:" how we preach, study, prophesy and most of all how we treat His people! If you notice, Sunday morning is one of the most segregated times for what we call "The Church." God didn't call for "The Church" to be separated, but to become one, as Jesus and the Father are one. That's what He wants every church that's standing in, and for His name to be (John 10:30). If we get this one thing right with God, how in the world are we going to get it right with the World?

Jesus came to seek and save those who are/were lost but He never stated a color, culture, race, economics, a community, or a neighborhood (Luke19:10). If the world can see color, economical differences, race and most of all favoritism or cliques in "The Church," don't you believe that God sees them as well? We as "The Church" can't do the same thing as the world and expect the World to come get help, deliverance and most of all, the Love that God left for "The Church." The reason some people don't come to "The Church" is because they see "The Church" doing the same thing as the world! We act like them, we talk like them, we dress like them, we conduct our business like them, but when we come in "The Church" we put on our church clothes, our church attitude, and our church voices while our hearts are far from Him (Matthews 15:8, Isaiah 29:13)!

Didn't the word tells us to come from among them and be yea separated says the Lord and once we do that then He will receive us and our offerings (2 Corinthians 6:17). We as "The Church" have to stop depending on the world system and start believing and depending on nothing else but the Word of God. Until "The Church" changes its mind frame from thinking about its own agenda and start focusing back on what God had preordained through His Word for it, no matter what "The Church" does; preach, prophesy, conducting conferences or workshops, Christmas parties, not only will it be out of order with God but it will not be successful. "The Church" really expects God to receive us when we don't realize His purpose and plan which should be about our Father's business.

"The Church" will know the "Truth," and the "Truth" will set you free (John 8:32). In "The Church" the only thing that the people really want to hear is the "Truth," to know the "Truth" and nothing but the truth. Not fables, lies, traditions, unusual doctrines, but God, Jesus and the Holy Ghost. We don't want to hear about the pastor, but the Word that God allows him to speak to the people. We don't want to hear about the pastors bragging or talking about the topics in the world because we know that. We are in the world but not of the world and it is going to take us to change them, not them changing us. We want Jesus to be ministered about His death, His burial and His Resurrections. That's what it is going to take to save us, to change the world, to change our children and like the church is saying, change the atmosphere. We as "The

Church" are tired of hearing about the lies about Christmas and how Jesus was in the manger with the Wiseman when the Word tells us He was 2 years old and in a house when the Wiseman brought the gold, Frankincense and myrrh (Matthews 2:11).

"The Church" never tells us that the shepherds were the ones that found him in the manger (Luke 2:8-15). Isn't it funny that we never read that Christmas was His birthday, and if it was His birthday why didn't we read it in the Bible that He celebrated it?

In the 4th Chapter of Galatians Paul wrote that he addressed the Galatians about turning their backs and worshipping dumb idols when they knew God (The Truth). Paul also stated that he was afraid of them (verses 8-11).

Also, we as "The Church," we are really tired on how you're trying to justify all these lies about Christmas, Easter, Halloween and any other paganism/demonic things that's going on in the house of God. For Halloween, "The Church" instead of telling the children the truth, disguised it as a Harvest Feast; Treats in a truck, but it's still the same and yet, we are supposed to be the salt of the Earth and if we're not careful we will lose its savor (Matthews 5:13-16). How can a person die on a Friday and 3 days later raise on a Sunday (Easter)?

"The Church" is so caught up on prosperity, the anointing, and numbers (members in the church) that we are missing God and the true anointing. Don't tell "The Church" how to get blessed. We know that if we pay our tithes and offerings, God will open the window of Heaven and pour out a blessing that we would not have room enough to receive (Malachi 3:8). We also know that if we give it shall be given press down, shaken together and running over shall men give from his bosom (Luke 6:38). We know that if we observe to do according to the Word of God and turn not to the left nor to the right that God will bless us wherever "The Church" goes (Joshua 1:7).

Some churches are so caught up on the fake anointing that they will try to do anything to obtain it true. The want the true anointing but they don't want to be saved, obedient nor subject to God's will (Acts 8:9-25). It's sad that "The Church" is compromising the Word just to get the church packed. Doesn't the Word tell us to preach the Word, be instant in season and out of season (2 Timothy 4:1-3)? Didn't Jesus tell Peter to feed the sheep? He asked Peter first, do you love me? Then He informed him to feed His sheep, don't love God's people because of feeding them they are hollering and pointing instead of teaching and instructing (John 21:17).

The Word isn't for everybody because not everybody, nor every church is going to obey God's commandments! But the congregation is asking for "The Church" to tell us, yes, tell us how to deal with us (Spirits)? Tell us, "The Church" how to deal with spiritual warfare because our fight is not with flesh and blood but against principalities; against powers and against the rulers of darkness in this world (Ephesians 6:12). Our fight is dealing with familiar spirits, demonic forces and by pulling down strongholds in my life. Its time out in "The Church" for Easter speeches when our children are dying in the streets. It's time out for singing these hip-hop songs in "The Church" when our daughters are getting pregnant in "The Church." It's time out for the excuses and playing in "The Church" when our families are dying, not knowing Christ in the midst of their sins. It's time out for the Christmas trees when "The

Church" can't feed the homeless during winter time. It's time out for all the foolishness that we, "The Church," are saying that we are doing in the name of our Lord and Savior Jesus Christ while actually lying and doing it for ourselves.

It's time for "The Church" to take back its rightful place, reclaim the authority that He has given it and to take responsibility to stand up for the truth without compromise.

Jesus is waiting for "The Church" to bring forth, to come forth and to be what God had made it to be. Jesus styled "The Church" like a woman that's impregnated with a seed. The Church is impregnated with the Word. Like a woman, she (The Church) goes through many things while waiting on the seed to manifest in child birth. She waits for 9-months for the birth, just like the day of Pentecost while they were in the upper room waiting for the "Promise" (Acts 2:1-4). While she (The Church) is waiting, the body goes through many transformations; the body goes through many forms, different spreads, many pains, trials, tribulations, different cravings, likes, dislikes and different mood swings, waiting on the day that the seed that was planted will come forth.

While she is waiting, she (The Church) has sleepless nights and prayers and talks to God for a smooth transformation. On that day when the pains increase and what's getting ready to come forth is almost ready to take her out; the pains are almost too hard to bear but the scripture states that He would not put any more than you can bare. Then you feel the breakthrough and the water breaks, it's almost that time, the water represents the baptism of the promise. Then she, "The Church," has to push out the manifestation. She has to push out the promises. She has to push out what God has promised. While she is waiting, The Church, does not stagger at the promises of God (Romans 4:20) so that when the baby, "The Church," comes forth, it doesn't have any deformities or defects and it is perfect in every way to stand up for God and His Word. Now, as you can see "The Church" has a great responsibility. The world, your family, job and children are not going to get any better until we (The Church) bring forth, get back in line and be what God has instructed us to be. If my people, (The Church) which are called by my name, shall humble themselves, pray, seek my face, and turn from their wicked ways then, will I hear from heaven, forgive their sins and will heal their land (2 Colossians 7:14). That's our answer to healing our lands. For our wives be submissive to their one husband and families bonding back with God. For all of these things that are going on in the World, we "The Church" have the answer. God is waiting on us to get in line, write a vision (Habakkuk 2:1) for His people, and bring back the Love that He had stored in "The Church" (John13:35).

The Word Ichabod (the glory of God has departed) will be written on the doorpost and not only will you not receive the promise, but you will not receive the paradise.

Too many times we want obligation. It's our responsibility to tell the "Truth" about God, Jesus and the Holy Ghost, not to get caught up in this world system, but the Word of God. We are not to get distracted from the purpose and the plans that God has given to "The Church" but use the Word to solve every situation, every disease and every problem that not only The Church has, but also the world.

God has given every church a purpose and a vision for their church, families', households', neighborhoods' and especially their communities'. For all these things that are going on in the World, we "The Church," have the answer. God is waiting on us to get in line. If you acknowledge God and ask Him to direct you, He will make it plain (Habakkuk 2:2). One of the main problems The Church is experiencing is we are allowing us to govern the House of God instead of God. The "Truth" nor the power of the truth is evident, nor manifested as a whole in "The Church" today. Since Jesus, which is the "Truth," is not being preached in our churches as a whole, we (The Church) have opened the doors.

Jesus Blesses.

"And Bezalel and Aholiab, and every gifted artisan in whom the Lord has put wisdom and understanding, to know how to do all manner of work for the service of the sanctuary, shall do according to all that the Lord has commanded."

Exodus 36:1

The Lord's Prayer
- Jesus

Our Father, who art in heaven, hallowed be thy Name,
thy kingdom come, thy will be done,
on earth as it is in heaven.

Give us this day our daily bread. And forgive us our trespasses, as we forgive those
who trespass against us.

And lead us not into temptation, but deliver us from evil.

For thine is the kingdom, and the power, and the glory, for ever and ever. Amen.

"But select capable men from all the people, men who fear God, trustworthy men who hate dishonest gain and appoint them as officials over thousands, hundreds, fifties and tens."

Exodus 18:21

Chapter Four
Pastors, False Prophets, False Teaching

Before I decided to write this chapter, I had to make sure that I was in line with God and the Word of God. So, after clearing my mind and allowing the Holy Ghost to lead and guide me to what I needed to say, the first words that I heard from God were, some apostles, prophets, bishops, pastors, evangelists and ministers are going to Hell and taking "My" people with them! They don't have the best interest for "My" people and are leading them astray by applying their doctrine and not the Word of truth. Some people's ideologies, their doctrines, and their way of doing things is according to their Word and not God's Word or God's will. They are making the Word of God to be of no effect through your traditions which you have handed down and many such things you do" (Mark7:13).

Instead of allowing My Word to cover My people, you're bringing more hurt to hurt and allowing paganism, covertness, and idol worshiping to cover My people. Jezebel spirits are possessing the pulpit and justifying the people's sins instead of allowing the Word to correct them.

Jezebel is not a male or female, it's a Demonic spirit. It can manipulate, control, be bitter, covert, witchcraft and last but certainly not least, a lying prophesying spirit. Telling My people that God understands and that He knows their hearts. I stated in My Word that I'll give them a new heart (Ezekiel 36:26) to take their hearts away from knowing me and My will. I will take away that heart of stone and give them a heart of flesh so that they will be able to accept me (The Word).

I commanded you to "Preach the Word" to be instant, in season and out of season, but what do you do? Instead of preaching the Word, you come up with deep revelations or some private interpretations (deceptions). You're chasing after the anointing but you don't want deliverance. Thus causing My people to error from the truth because you want to hold on to your traditions and dead works. You talk to My people more about the problems in the world instead of telling them that they are in the world, but not of the world (John 17:16). You never tell them to Sanctify (set apart) them by My truth; My Word is truth (John 17:17).

Set themselves from the lies, the fables the things that have them bound and the things that have them oppressed. Preach My son, Jesus, and how He set the captives that were in captivity Free (Luke 4:18). Just preach the Word. Stop trying to set up your Kingdom, thinking you're some great wonder and telling the men and women that this is My house but you are self-appointed and the spirit of Ichabod rest of the door mantel.

To cast spirits but not in My name, trying to save souls but it's not of Me; your hidden agenda is money (Matthews 6:24). You're God out in your songs, which you state that I told you to write but when you don't get the air play, or Grammy's, or the money you thought you should have gotten, then you go to the world systems. Then you have the audacity to say that I can't judge you, but your actions and attitude have already judged you. Now in your programs, and even in your messages, how many times do you tell My people that I'm a Healer, Deliverer and can make every crooked path straight (Luke3:5)? You state that they are from me but they are not.

The messages that you preach are bringing My people into more condemnation than setting them free. Moses to walk perfect before me. I perfected Enoch that he became a friend of mine and yet he walked to heaven with me, telling my people that no one is perfect but Jesus. I informed and I also left in My Word to mark the perfect man (Psalms 37:37). True, you all state that it was Jesus, but there are still some perfect men and women that are on the earth now (Be yea perfect as your Father is heaven is perfect Matthews 5:48).

If that were not the case I would have never had it written that I'm coming back from a church without a spot, wrinkle, blemish or any such thing other than perfection and completeness (Ephesians 5:27). Thus you have left your first love (Rev 2:4) so I have against you and you're allowing the devil to deceive you by allowing the works of the flesh (Galatians 5:19-21) to operate in My house instead of the fruits of the Spirit.

Just because you preach my word, you think that I have called you but that I have called you, but everyone that's called isn't called by Me! You see, people look at the outward appearances but not only do I look at the heart, (1 Samuel 16:7) but I also weigh the heart to see if he has the endurance, the strength and wisdom to minister to My people. Not everyone that states that they are mine are mine, but are ministers of deceit and deception. They are leading the people astray because they don't study nor the ministers that are ministering to them. "Woe to the shepherds who are destroying and scattering the sheep of My pastures!" Says the Lord (Jeremiah 23:1). Therefore thus says the Lord, "God of Israel against the shepherds who feed My people, you have scattered My flock driven them away and not attended to them. Behold, I will attend to them. Behold, I will attend to you for the evil doings," says the Lord. "But I will gather the remnants of My flock out of all countries where I have driven them and bring them back to their folds. And they shall be fruitful and increase.

I will set up shepherds over them who will feed them and they shall fear no more, nor be dismayed, nor shall they be lacking." Says the Lord (Jeremiah 23:1-4).

There are many things that I would like to write but God has informed me to leave the Word; the Bible; the book of instructions to instruct you to guide His people to the true word. Also, for you to minister to His people and to not go to the left nor to the right but preach what has informed you; not what you hear, not what you think, not your ideologies, but His Word.

God also informed me to tell you all, that He sees the Leaders that are having sex in the churches and allowing their sons and daughters to do it as well. He informed me to read what He did to Samuel and his sons (1 Samuel 2:12-36). He also informed me to tell you, He sees the money changers. The money changers that are in the House of God and He told me to ask you all do you remember what He did in the book of Matthews (21:13)? He said to them, "It is written. My house shall be called a house of prayer, but you have made it a den of thieves." Proverbs (16:18), Pride goes before destruction and a haughty spirit before a fall. This is the warning that God allowed me to read to His leaders: get it straight with Him, regardless of what people in the congregation, friends or family have to say.

You have a charge to keep and a God to glorify (Leviticus 8:35). So, if you are called by His name and you found yourself coming short, then repent so the "Real Church of God" (2 Corinthians 7:14) can stand up with power, boldness and the anointing that God has for you and the place where He has you.

In Jesus' Mighty Name Amen

"But those who wait on the Lord shall renew their strength, they shall mount up with wings like eagles, they shall run and not be weary, they shall walk and not faint."

Isaiah 40:31

A Psalm of David

The Lord is my shepherd; I shall not want.

He makes me to lie down in green pastures; He leads me beside the still waters.

He restores my soul;
He leads me in the paths of righteousness For His name's sake.

Yea, though I walk through the valley of the shadow of death, I will fear no evil;
For You are with me;
Your rod and Your staff, they comfort me.

You prepare a table before me in the presence of my enemies; You anoint my head with oil;
My cup runs over.

Surely goodness and mercy shall follow me All the days of my life; And I will dwell[a] in the house of the Lord Forever.

Psalm 23

Chapter Five
TRADITIONS

The traditions of men instead of the Word of God are in questioned. We as the "Real Church of God," have to stand up. Traditions, handing down statements, beliefs, legends and customs from generation to generation by word of mouth or by practice but have no merits, nor are they spiritually based or Biblical, if God is not in it. Too many times we allow the traditions of man and the sayings to supersede the Word of God. We give more respect, reverence and more hearing than actually seeing, looking or researching to see if the tradition is true. Does it have any merit and does it line up with God's will or His word?

God has given us the ability and the power to cast down every tradition that we allow to be built up in our lives by reading His Word, studying the Word of God and asking the Holy Ghost to help you in areas that we are struggling with or in.

If traditions aren't Biblical nor spiritually based, then they're demonic. Anything that you allow to enter the house of God or in your spirit, which is Holy, that is not Holy, defiles the Word of God or the power of God and is against God is demonic. Traditions, trying to get God to do what He already has done through His Word by the works of our flesh. Trying to make Him (God) do through disbelief, he said she said, vain reputations, sacrifices, log prayers, customs, generation to generation. Traditions have separated us from getting the true anointing that God has for us. It has limited us from getting the spiritual foods, God preordained we have in our lives.

Tradition can stunt our growth with God. It has also stunted our real relationship that we have with our heavenly Father and if you're not careful, traditions will have you rebel against God and His Word. Rebel, yes, rebel when someone tells you what thus states the Lord through His Word and you reject it by reading it or seeing it. You don't reject that person that stated or showed you the Word but you rejected God through His Word. Too many times you will hear people state, "I don't care what it says, I know the Bible for myself." Or do you know tradition? In reality you're refusing corrections, you're refusing to have that yoke broken and you're refusing the Holy Ghost to bless you. It (Tradition) has caused division with you and God's will; division with you and the Holy Ghost. It's a division between the truth and a lie (you shall know the truth and the truth shall set you free John 8:32).

Traditions have destroyed our relationship with God, to the church, to you and back to God. Tradition and insanity aren't they the same thing? Tradition is doing the same thing year after year, time after time and expecting a different result. Insanity is doing the same thing over and over and expecting a different result. Basically, they're the same thing. Traditions will have you saying things that are contrary to you, your life and the will that God can have for you. For example, I could have been dead and sleeping in my grave but Did God not state that when you were in your mother's womb, He knew you? And that if God knew you, He would set a path for your life? So stop saying traditional things to condemn you and your life. Start speaking life into your situation and not death.

So, if it were meant for you to be on drugs, you would have. If it were meant for you to die in that wreck, you would have. If it were meant for you to marry that person, you would have. If it were meant for you to be this or to do that, do you know you would have?

Stop speaking over your life that you're climbing on the rough side of the mountain (Traditions) and speak to your mountain. The Word says it shall be moved. Stop saying that I was born a certain religion and that's what I'm going to be (tradition). You were born Holy and the Bible states, Holy you shall be. You decided to practice that certain religion without asking God. Stop allowing the traditions that we practice on a day to day basis, dictate to you, your beginning and your ending.

We used to state that if we stepped on a crack, we would break our mother's back. Well I know some of you all have stepped on a lot of cracks, but did your mother's back crack? That same mind frame about backs being cracked is brought into the church and if we are not careful, not only will that leave us with a traditional mind frame but that will not be good for God nor yourself.

Look at how we come to church, have to sit in the same seat every Sunday or whenever you attend (Tradition), unless you are assigned that seat or that area, and you get an attitude when someone else sits there. Look at the same service every Saturday or Sunday nothing changes; same time for offerings, the choir and the service to end. I realize that the Word states that everything has to be decent and in order, but have you ever stopped the tradition and allowed the Holy Ghost to lead and guide you in the service?

There is a scripture in the Bible that says the spirit was so high that it filled the temple and that the Word of God was not ministered (1 Kings 8:11). You have to understand that your ways are not God's ways when you're in traditions nor are your thoughts His thoughts (Isaiah 55:8).

Why at some churches when you go to give your life to God and get saved, you go up, they ask you if you want to be filled with the Holy Ghost, you say yes and they tell you to say a Word or something until you start saying something that sounds like tongues and then they stated that you have it (Traditions)?

True you can receive the Holy Ghost by laying of hands but also in the book of Acts, the disciples tarried until they were endured with power. That means God cannot dwell in an unclean temple. He has to get uncleanliness out before He (Holy Ghost) comes in. That's why some people have a form of God (Tradition) and can do all the things in the church and around it but they have no power, no evidence and no deliverance. They're acting out in their own flesh. Let's say it together, TRADITION.

Listen to our songs that we sing in church. Singing traditions that no yokes are being broken and no deliverance but a lot of Flesh. It's getting to the point where the church songs are not talking or singing about Jesus, but flesh. Saying He knows, He saves (Who's "he?" "He" can be anybody). If you're singing about Jesus, just say Jesus.

Do me a favor, listen to the song that is in the atmosphere, "I need just a little more Jesus." True, that individual might need Jesus but you might not. What you need is more studying, reading the Word and asking God to help in the area of unbelief.

Another song is, "We fall down but we get up." True statement but it's a verse that stated, "A saint is a sinner who fell down and got up." False statement; that's deception and a trick of the enemy. Last song: in this song, I believe there is a verse that states, "the devil peeped into your future." The devil is not omnipresent and he can't do that. If that was possible, he would have prevented you from being saved. He would have stopped Jesus from being manifested.

If we are not careful, we will come to church heavy burdened and leave the same way. It is time that the "Real Church of God" come against the traditions of the church to cast the wicked images that seem to have us bound. Our traditions have put everything in front of God and His Word. The reason I'm saying this is to ask, "You" (Traditions of the church) put God (Holy Ghost) on a program? You give or put the Word of God on a schedule, a time limit, so we can do us (flesh) rather than hearing the Word of God. Think about it, the average time the church is spending hearing or reading the Word of God is about 30 minutes. The average time for singing and praise dancing is over 30 minutes. People will stay for the praise and worship service but don't want to hear the Word. Isn't that backwards. Say it with me, "Traditions."

It is time we break the traditions that we have built within us and the church. The Word of God is more important than any song and without the Word, there would not be any praise, praise dancing or worship. The devil knows, if this very tradition that we overlook, is practiced in every church, not only would we come to church for the wrong reason and motives but, we will slowly loose the anointing that God has placed upon our lives.

This a form of distraction that the devil is bringing in the church, "traditions." There should not be anything more important than the glory of God's presence through His Word. True, we use the singing and praise dancing to usher in the presence or the anointing of God in the temples but we should bring that with us when we come to church.

Now if we allow our lives and the Word of God to penetrate us on a daily basis and come into His temple or presence on one accord, you would feel the move of God like never before. You talk about yokes being broken, bodies being healed, marriages being mended back together and family members starting getting saved. My God, my God. You talk about the captives being set free. You're talking about a high time in the Lord but the traditions of men, instead of the Word of God has stopped us from true worship. We have to break those traditions and start standing on the Word of God. If you don't understand, ask the Holy Ghost for understanding. We as the church leaders, have covet other people's traditions instead of reading it or acknowledging God to do a certain thing. We build ourselves up on other people's traditions, ideals and beliefs. Did God tell you to get praise dancers? Did He tell you to view other men or women ministers? Did not God tell you to write out a vision for your church and your life? Did He not say to make it plain (Habakkuk 2:2)? So, why are you caught up on all these traditions? If God told you to build it, will He not equip it?

Let's view the praise dancing. Almost every church you attend now has them. Every church that you attend spends more time with praise dance. Many praise dancers don't know the purpose of dancing in praise. David danced when the Ark of the Convent came back to the children of Israel (2 Samuel 6, 1 Chronicle 15:29), but now we do praise singing and fleshly activities in the Word of God. Can you say this is "Tradition?" We as the church have allowed everything and anything to minister to us, other than the real Word of God. We have allowed and brought in every tradition to the house of God. We have allowed events and others such as; Easter, Eastern Star, Masonic, Halloween, Christmas, Mama saying and grandma's beliefs. every tradition and belief under the hands of men. Then now if a person doesn't read or doesn't study the Word of God he will be easily offended. The scriptures state, "You leave the commandments of God and hold to the tradition of men" (Mark 7:8).

As the "Real Church of God," we have to stand up. We have to be very careful of the traditions that are coming into the house of God. We have been so used to the traditions of men, that we make the Word of God of no effect (useless) (Mark 7:13). So, it is time we cast down the traditions of men that are plaguing our churches so that the real anointing/power of God can come in, deliver and set free the people of God. Some of these traditions have set up witchcraft (disobedience) in the church and the people that attend the church. When the truth is preached or read, we as the church fight against it. Thus, causing the Word to not deliver or set free the men and women of God.

Traditions: Customs or beliefs that have been carried on from generation to generation. Some have no spiritual or Biblical base.

We have allowed the world's way of thinking, doing or saying to infest the church. Watch night service? What does that really have to do with New Year service?

Did not the Bible say, "Esteeming one day over another?" (Romans 14:5) Has anyone really looked into watch service and what it really means? Lie or tradition? Are we so based on traditions that we would rather believe the lie or tradition than the truth? Watch service, aka "Freedom Eve" is when the slaves went from house to house and some in the church, waiting for the Emancipation Proclamation to be signed in 1862. They were not praying on New Year's, but hoping and praying that they would be freed. So true, they prayed to God but not about the New Year to come but that the bill would be signed and they would be set free. If a person that doesn't participate in New Year's Eve service (Watch night) because they know that they are set free and know the truth then why are they criticized, belittled and talked about? Only in the black churches, do they practice such traditions. But the funniest tradition that I have heard, is eating black eyed peas on New Year's for good luck. So, if a person doesn't eat or like black eyed peas, does that mean they will be cursed for that year or every year for the rest of their lives? Did not the Word say that God is not to be mocked and that whatever a man sows, he will also reap? So, if you sow good seed (regardless of the black-eyed peas), then you shall reap good seeds. So, if that is the case (what history stated), why are we still praying that God will set us free?

My former pastor made a statement saying, "regardless of you praying for the following year to come in, if it is God's will, it is going to come."

Easter; what do Easter baskets, Easter eggs, buying new clothes to attend services or the bunny rabbit have to do with the death, burial and resurrection of Jesus Christ? True, the rabbit represents fertility when Jesus died. We became the newness of life through His death but that is all. Also, how do you get 3 days from Friday to Sunday? Three days Jesus stayed in the grave. So, if He died on a Friday, he rose on a Sunday? I'm not the smartest person but that's not three days. We can talk about it or get our minds all in knots but you can't get those days to come up to 3 (Friday - Sunday). True, the word of Easter is in the book of Acts, but it's really dealing with Esther the Canaanite Goddess (Acts 12:1-4).

Christmas; it amazes me that this day is supposed to be Jesus Christ's birthday but you never heard of Him celebrating it nor do you read about it in the Bible. In Luke the 1st chapter and 26th verse it tells you, in the 6th month (June) that the Holy Ghost leaped in Mary. So, if the Bible states the 6th month (June), and it takes 9-months for the baby to fully develop. So, let me see 6 months plus 9-months for a fully developed baby, that gives us 15. There are 12 months in a year (our modern-day calendar). Then we have 3 months left over, so that's March. But if we use the Jewish calendar, that's 13 months. Then we have 2 months left over and that gives us February. So, anyway you look at it, there is no way that Jesus could have been born in December.

Also, do me a favor, look up Christmas or December 25th. It will state that it's a pagan holiday (pagans were people that didn't like God and fought against His Word). Christmas trees in the book of Jeremiah in the 10th chapter of the Bible states that this was a tradition that the pagan people did not state that they are saved by or know God.

If you read Luke the 2nd chapter, around the 8th verse it tells us that the shepherds were attending the sheep when Jesus was born. You might be saying it was a different temperature there but no. When it's cold here, it's also cold over there. The book of Matthews 2nd chapter, verse 11 tells us when the wise men came to Jesus that He was in a house, not a manger. It was never stated that there were 3 wise men but the gifts that were presented were gold, frankincense and mirth.

Halloween; Why do we still have that in the church? Just because they don't celebrate it in the streets, going from house to house, you have it in the church (demonic). That day, yes Halloween, is the day that they persecuted the saints. Yes, killed the saints. You dress up in masks (Demonic) and go from house to house. Read the book of Acts. They went house to house to persecute/kill believers. They brought out saints and killed them for worshiping Jesus. The ones that did such deeds, were rewarded for their deeds (treats). Our traditions have taken us away from what the Holy Ghost is really trying to get us to understand. Did not the scripture say that once God had set us free that we are free and freed indeed (John 8:36)? So why are we doing what keeps us bound? Didn't the scripture state that you shall know the truth and the truth shall set you free? So why are we doing things that are a lie (Tradition) and have us bound? Some have witchcraft embedded in them (John 8:32).

We are "The Real Church of God," how can we bring people to church so that Jesus can show them truth when you, yourself are caught up on traditions?
Jesus Bless

Chapter Six
Deceptions

For many deceivers have entered the world. They are those that do not confess that Jesus Christ is coming in the flesh? This mentality or perspective is caused by the deceiver and the Antichrist (2 John 1:7). The devil has brought so much confusion in the land, in the churches, in our lives with various TV shows, traditions, worldly sayings, etc. If you're not careful, he will have you thinking and believing that God/Jesus isn't real nor is His Holy Word. Here are some of the deceptions and confusion that the devil has planted in our minds. The modern Church and the Devil is deceiving us because we have put down the Bible or God's Word and started looking at him (Devil) and his deceptive methods.

Before we start in this chapter, let's take a moment and see what the Word deception or to be deceived means. Deception is, the act of making someone believe in something that's not true; beguilement deceit, bluff mystification and subterfuge is the act of propagating belief in this that are not true, or not the whole truth (as in half-truth omission). The word deceive means: to mislead by a false appearance or statement delude.

Thus, we are allowing the deception and the deceiving nature of the world to tell us that there is no one perfect but God. Anytime you take one word, especially in a phrase from the Word of God, and change one word; one meaning; one saying to justify your purpose, it changes the entire meaning of what was originally written. Whenever you hear a word, statement or phrase and you allow it to minister to you. It gets in your spirit and it emboldens you.

When you don't study what has been planted in your spirit or what you have heard and do not research that topic, you don't learn what you were supposed to learn. Then you decide to share that information to others trying to make them believe what was spoken or what you heard. We hear it in the songs. If you're not careful, you'll say it and we even hear it in our churches but what does the Word say if the only ones that are perfect are God, Jesus and the Holy Ghost? If that was the case, why did the Bible say to Mark the perfect man (Psalms 37:37)? You may have heard that they were talking about Jesus and God at the time. Well, if that's the case then why did God allow His word in the Bible to call Job a perfect and upright man that fears God and shun evil (Job 1:2)? Then, Jesus bragged on Job in that same chapter in verse 8. When Satan came to present himself, Jesus said that there was none like him (Job); a prefect and upright. That was Jesus bragging on Job. Did not God tell Abram to walk before Him (God) perfect? So, if he had to walk before God perfectly, it means he had to be perfect (Genesis17:1). Still not totally convinced?

Jesus commanded us to "Be ye perfect as your Father which is in heaven is perfect" (Mathews 5:48). Also, Jesus stated that He (Jesus) is coming back for a church without a spot, wrinkle or blemish or any such thing (Ephesians 5:27). So, if He's coming back for a church without spot, wrinkle or blemish, then He commands you to be perfect.

You and I know that we have to be perfect or striving to be perfect to not only to be called Christian, but you have to be perfect to make it in that perfect place called heaven. Paul was a man like unto us made a powerful statement. He said that He was perfect but was striving for a higher calling in Christ Jesus (Philippians 3:14). Perfect only means to be complete in an area or a topic; not having a spot, wrinkle or blemish. Have you ever taken a test in school or college where you made a perfect score of 100%? That is a perfect score. So, God does have perfect people in this world, but they are perfect in the blood of Jesus. In their perfection, they overcome trials, tribulations, stresses of this world by the blood of the Lamb and by the words of their testimonies. Stop allowing people to deceive you by telling you that the only one who is perfect, is God/ Jesus. If that were the case, Jesus wouldn't allow perfection to be classified with us, God/ Jesus, His Word and the Holy Ghost.

Just like you have to strive to enter in the straight gate, you have to allow the blood to clean you up from all infirmities of the flesh and spirit. Also, allow His Word and the Holy Ghost to complete or perfect the work and will that God has for your life.

Another form of deception is when we think we can do something and don't think that repercussion will occur. Whatever you sow is going to come back to you in a reaping form. Too many times people would sow chaos, gossip, trouble and turmoil not only in their lives but in others. Then they have the audacity to question God when the reaping season comes. You're not only going to reap trouble, it can also effect and affect your family (Galatians 6:7-8). Too many times we sit back, wondering why things are going wrong for us. We wonder why so much trouble is happening in our lives or in our families. Just take a moment and ask God, "What's the problem?" Don't get me wrong, sometimes it could be that the devil is buffing you but if you really seek God, He will show you that there's some stuff you have sown a while back or maybe years ago. You never repented, or got it right with an individual, or a situation and now it's coming back to you but in a different form. Just like David when he had Uriah killed because he wanted Bathsheba. This type of event not only affected his kingdom, but its effecting us now. God said, "Since David sowed in ungodliness, he would reap ungodliness." There was a division in his household and not only that, there has been war to this day (2 Samuel 11). Do me a favor and read about David's household once he reaped ungodliness. His son slept with one of his wives, daughter got raped by her brother and son got killed. You can read all of this in 2 Samuel and 1 Kings. Just think, David was a man after God's own heart and even though he repented, asked God to clean him up but there were repercussions. His fall was a very great fall. That is one of the deceptions, lies and manipulations that the devil has in the world. Yes, it's in our churches and its effecting and affecting our lives.

Another one of the deceptions that the devil tries to get you to believe and accept, is that we all serve the same God. But didn't the Bible say, "For even there are so called gods, whether in heaven or on earth (as there are many gods and many lords). 1 Corinthians 8:5. The devil is trying to bring that same manipulative spirit into the church. Some of us have been taught that reading or studying our Bible is what allows the devil and his pastor/ministers to tell the church and God's people that we serve the same God. That's one form of the Anti-Christ and we are allowing this to impact the house of God. Let's think about this for a moment before we continue in this chapter. If we are serving the same God, why are there so many different churches, different religions and different denominations? Why are there different ways of teaching/preaching, praying, worshiping, different ways, different days to enter God's house to worship, different ways to minister and most of all different ways to reach God, if we all are serving the same God? Then why do some churches believe in one thing and another church doesn't believe in another, if we serve the same God? Some believe in the whole Bible, some in the full gospel and some in either Old or New Testament. Why do some religions say that their way is the only way to get to God and others state that theirs is the way? The devil brings this confusion because we don't read, we don't study, and we don't ask God to show us the truth about Him and His word. Instead we seek man in place of God and that's how the devil is able to deceive you. By making us think we serve the same God. So why do some kill and say they are doing it for God? The word states, "revenge is mine and I shall repay," says the Lord (Romans 12:19).

So, no we don't serve the same God. Nor do we worship Him (Jesus) the same, or in the spirit of Holiness. Stop allowing the devil to put/plant those seeds in your mind, in your spirit and in your heart. There are many deceivers and gods in our lands lust like there are many deceivers in our churches. Some are saying that there's no God, and Jesus wasn't born of a virgin, to the point that He wasn't the Son of God. One way that we deceive ourselves or are being misconceived is when we believe that if we accept Jesus as our personal Savior or just go to church and pay tithes, that we are going to heaven. That's another big deception that we can deceive ourselves with the Bible. The Bible says that if we don't have the spirit of Christ (Holy Ghost) then we are none of His (Romans 8:9). So, you can play the part of being Holy, you may even act the part (Holy) but you're only deceiving yourself because if you're not trying to do what God commanded you to do and if you are not working on yourself, it's not going to work. Also, there is a scripture that states that if we name the name of the Lord, then we depart from iniquity (2 Timothy 2:19). So, don't think or allow someone to plant a seed in your mind that once you're saved, you're always saved or that once you receive Christ, that you are a shoe in to go to heaven. That's not the right way of thinking nor does the Bible say that. The Bible states that you have to deny yourself, to pick up your cross daily and follow after our Lord and Savior, Jesus Christ (Luke 9:23).

You can't allow the world or anyone that's in it, to cause you to stray away from God and His Word. Another way that we are deceiving ourselves, when we tell ourselves that if you're anointing and the spirit of God is on you or around you, you can't go to hell (Wrong). If God has blessed you, and His presence is on or around you, but you start practicing sin, unrighteousness and iniquity, then God's anointing will not rest on you anymore until you start doing God's will again. Don't get me wrong, if God has given you a gift and or a talent, His gifts are without repentance (Romans 11:29). But He will not allow His spirit to rest, rule and abide in or around you until you repent. What if you, or another person, die while you are in the midst of sin? Then what? No matter how good your righteousness is, you may want to consider how many souls you brought to Christ, or how many messages you ministered. Once you refuse to practice God's will and do what His Word informs you to do, all of your righteousness will not be remembered anymore.

Some people think and believe that the gifts that God has blessed them with are going to save them (Deception). Your gifts don't save you. Nor do they deliver you. Gifts that God gives to an individual are given freely; solely for His purpose and His plan. Another deception is when we state that we can agree to disagree.

Wow, that's not sound thinking. Too many times we try to compromise with God's Word, with His will and commandments. God's Word, is God's Word. It doesn't need to be added to, justified, or watered down to fit you. The Word is meant to fix you. Basically, it's saying that you don't want, hear nor heed corrections.

Nor do you want anyone to correct you on how you feel and what you believe. I never read in the Bible that God compromised with the people of Israel and said that He will agree to disagree with you. God's word is right and if you don't agree with it or accept it, then you know where your end will be. So, if you know something that you read in His Word; something that God has spoken to you then don't compromise with what the devil states. Quote what God has said. Don't agree to disagree, that's compromising. Just believe in what God has placed in you and if they don't believe the truth, just pray for them.

Shake the very dusk from among you. There are several other forms of deception. One is a lie, another is manipulation and another one is deceiving yourself. Yes, you can deceive yourself. The Bible reminds us to "Lie not to one another, seeing that ye have put off the old man with his deeds; and have put on the new which is renewed in knowledge (Colossians 3:9-10)." True, we know that people in the world are going to lie. If they are unsaved, they are going to do unsaved things. But why do people say they know God, they are Christians, they are saved and sanctified but then they lie so much? Too many times in church we lie from everything to Pastors/leaders misleading the people, to not studying the Word of God and rightly dividing the Word of truth (2 Timothy 2:15), to telling one another I will call in 10 minutes, or I'll do this, or I'll do that and never do what you have said. That's a lie.

Another is when you don't study and ask God to lead and guide you. He wants you to minister from God to His people. Then you minister, even try to prophesize and the one speaking knows they didn't hear from God but are speaking from emotions. Not only are they lying to God's people, but also deceiving themselves (John 16:13).

We are doing what we want instead of what God's desires for His people. We wonder why the church and the people, aren't doing what God informed us or why the church isn't growing. And you're wondering where the anointing is and where God is. Now you know that lying carries a spirit of deception. When you engage in being deceptive you are going to find, people will get to the point that they don't trust you and they will hate to see you come but love to see you go. The spirit of lying is one of the things that God hates. God does love you but if you're operating in that deceptive spirit of lying (Proverbs 6:16-19), it causes a disconnection.

The thing about deception or being deceived is people don't know that they are deceived until they are in it too deep. Once they read or see that they are doing or saying something that is not true or scripturally based, there is a disconnection from God. Sometimes they wrestle with the truth until they cause their own hurt instead of repenting and getting it right with you and God. They will continue to justify the deception, saying that its right and makes you think or feel that you're wrong rather than the deception. Today, our modern day churches are operating under a lot of deception. If the people of God aren't careful, reading, studying and acknowledging God in everything that they do, they can be deceived (Matthews 24:24).

People deliberately deceive an individual for selfish gain or just to make someone think he/she knows something, and in reality they know nothing. So, if you start off deceiving people with lies, don't be surprised when people lie to you. There are so many deceptions in the modern day church with pastors and leaders are lying, manipulating, deceiving and being deceptive that the word Ichabod has been written on some of the churches doorpost.

Here are several more deceptions that are dominating our churches; some that I wanted or decided to point out. Nowhere in the Bible, was Christmas written about. Nor did it (The Bible) tell us to celebrate Christmas. Neither is it true that Christmas is Jesus' Birthday. Didn't the Word say, "not to add, not to subtract from the Word, and if you do God will add to him the plagues that are written in this book. If you subtract from the book of prophecy that God shall take away his prat from the Book of Life (Revelation 22:19).

Also, you state it's a day that is set aside to celebrate and to give Jesus presents and glory. Nay; nope, it was a pagan holiday that was set aside to worship the sun, not the son. Pagans were people that made themselves gods because they didn't want to worship the true and living God. So once again, how, can you say it is in the Bible that it was Jesus' birthday? You never heard about Him (Jesus) celebrating it. In Luke 1:26- 39, it says in the six months an angle came. So, for six months; that's June and it takes nine months to have a baby. So that's 15 (6 months, the angel came 9 months to have a baby), (verse 44, the baby leaped in her stomach and that was the 6th month) then the bible says that Jesus was in a house when the wise men came (Matthews 2:11). Where do you get that there were 3 wise men? Nowhere in the Bible does it say there were three wise men. It says there were 3 gifts that were presented to Jesus (Gold, frankincense's and myrrh Matthews 2:11). So, when the wise men with the 3 gifts presented those gifts to Jesus, they came to His house not the manger, but His house. Also, the Bible says that the shepherds where there when He was born, (Luke 2:8-20) not the wise men.

Also, the Bible tells us not to be like the pagans when it comes to Christmas trees (Jeremiah 10:1-5). Now there is Easter. Yes, it's in the Bible, in the book of Acts. So, explain to me how a person can die on a Friday and rise on a Sunday, but yet its considered to be 3 days? That's not mathematically correct, so where do we get all these differences from? Let God's Word be true and every man be a liar (Romans 3:4).

So, where do we get Santa Claus and the Easter bunny? Not only are these pagan, but they're deceptions and if you're practicing them and telling people these lies, you are going to be held accountable for the deceit. At one time churches didn't celebrate Halloween, but since the world is putting pressure on the church, we accept the demonic things that it possesses. Just think; dressing up like witches, warlocks, ghost, and goblins to petition you for some tricks. Some churches try to cover it up and say it's a harvest feast but you do it at the same time as Halloween. You also pass out candy and some churches tell you to dress up in nice costumes but it's the same thing because it goes against God's Word, God's will and they're traditions of men instead of the Word of God.

Paul made a great statement that caused us to think deeply about our faith, when that you serve days and months and seasons and years. Paul stated, "I'm afraid of you (Galatian 4:8-12)." In that scripture, Paul was talking about Holidays; worshiping like harvest feast, Halloween, treat in a trunk, etc.

God has brought you all out of these deceptions (demonic practices) once you got saved. So why did you get back involved with the yoke of bondage by worshiping/ celebrating these days? Manipulation is to control or play upon by an artful, unfair, or insidious means; especially to one's own advantage.

If we state that we are God's children and if you're not following what thus stated the Lord, then not only are you deceived, but you are deceiving God's people.

I've learned over the years there is more deception in the churches than typically discussed. Like with Noah; how he brought 7 clean and 2 unclean of the animals in the ark but we have only been told that it was 2 of each kind. But they did walk 2 by 2 on the ark.

So, if after reading this chapter and the scriptures, you find yourself in error, repent and ask God to open your understanding. Ask Him to allow His spirit to deliver you from these deceptions that have been plaguing you, your family and even the church that you are or have been attending. It's time for you, me and the real Church of God to shake ourselves from the deceptions that are plaguing our churches. Also, to take a stand like never before! God is waiting on us to get it right with Him, so we can change the world.

In Jesus' Mighty name (Amen)

Chapter Seven
Lifting up the name of Jesus

Oh, that men would give thanks to the Lord for His goodness, and for His wonderful works to the children of men (Psalms 107:8).

To lift up means to raise, elevate, get up, bring up, raise from a lower to a higher position. Too many times in our personal lives, we lift up everything but Jesus. We lift up our jobs, our promotions and the amount of money we make, but did you know that promotions come from God? Promotions neither come from the east, from the west nor from the south. But God is the judge. He puts down one and exalts another (Psalms 75:6-7). Also, Jesus gave you the ability to gain wealth, to get that Job, the ability to get up and go to work, to buy your house, the cars and the clothes that you wear (Deuteronomy 8:18).

Some of you lift up your spouse more than you lift Jesus, but wasn't it Jesus that allowed you to marry your Boaz or your Ruth (Ruth 2)? Jesus wants to be elevated, raised up higher than your jobs, money, cars, spouses and even your houses. He allowed you to obtain and to sustain these things for your everyday need and even your desire. Some of you that go to church have the tendency of lifting up your positions and even your pastors more than you do Jesus. Giving more honor and respect to your leader that speaks about the Savior. Isn't that kind of backwards? They will praise and worship the creature more than the creator (Romans 1:25). Even during our holidays we give more respect and attention to them, than we do Jesus. For example, we lift up the Easter speeches, Easter bunny, Easter eggs, wearing new clothes and wearing new hats more than we do with the death, burial and resurrection of Jesus Christ. Have you considered what it meant for Him to die for us, to give His life for you and I? What about Christmas, a day that the world set aside for His birth? But look how we celebrate it, we give more honor and respect to the presents that we get, than the day that's set aside. On Christmas the people who celebrate, appear to be more selfish than at any other time of the year, but Jesus was unselfish. Looking at what they receive more than receiving the gift of life that Jesus has given to us all. Not understanding the scripture when it was stated that it is more blessed to give than receive (Acts 20:35).

On Thanksgiving Day we give more honor to the (pig) Ham or Turkey, for giving up their lives so we can have a happy food day. Rather than giving thanks unto the Lord, for He is good: for His mercy endured forever (Psalms 107:1).

Now the Church has adopted Halloween and we have given more honor to the candy, than Jesus. But have you not read where it is written that Jesus is sweeter than the honey on a honey comb (Psalms 119:103)? Also, we lift up and magnify our children, our sicknesses and yes, even the devil more than Jesus. But you shouldn't exalt, make big or elevate anyone and I mean anyone, not even God, over Jesus. The bible says, if Jesus (not God) be lifted-up, He (Jesus) will draw all men unto who (not God) but Jesus. You can't call Jesus Lord without the Holy Ghost revealing it to you (1 Corinthians 12:1); to show you who He really is, what part He played in your life and in the spiritual realm.

If you look at the Old Testament and see the word Lord God, what do you think they were talking about? Yes, and know what they were really saying and talking about, was Jesus. The word Lord, means Jesus. So that's Jesus in the image of God. Since Jesus wasn't manifested (born) at that time, God allowed men to write Lord God until He become manifested in the flesh. Now you see, study and understand why God allowed all power and authority to be in place, in the name of Jesus. You will never have a prefect praise or worship until you know why we lift up Jesus, and not God. True, God is our Father and maker of all things, but when you go against the Word of God and start worshiping God, instead of Jesus, then you violate the principals of the law and of the bible. Nowhere, have you read that God be lifted up, but it's Jesus be lifted-up, then He (Jesus) would draw all men unto Who? The Father. Why do you think that yoke isn't destroyed, bodies are not being healed and why people aren't coming to the house of God? Even in our Gospel songs we will ask, do you know Him? Or state that He's good, but Him could be anybody and he's good can be anybody as well. When you call on the name of Jesus, the devil trembles when you call that name.

Yokes we become broken when you believe in His name and you talk about families being delivered and set free. It's only going to happen when you lift up the name of Jesus. Let me explain to you how personal it is to God to lift up His son. There was or ever could be anyone worthy enough to redeem men back to the father. At that time there was no one to destroy the works of the devil, nor was there anyone that could set the captives free. So, God (The Father) allowed Jesus to be born through a virgin, (Mary) to come to earth and redeem us to the Father. God has given us His only begotten son; the son of the Father to come from heaven to a sinful world where he was lied on and persecuted for the likes of us.

Let's make this a little more personal so you can feel/understand what God really had to go through. How many of us would allow our only son to die for a nation/people that weren't worthy of His Grace, His mercy or His love. But God so loved us, that He allowed His son to give His life so that we might have the right to the tree of life. He came to His own, and they received Him not (John 1:11-13), to be rejected by His own. He came preaching the truth so that we can know the truth and the truth could set us free. The truth is Jesus (John 8: 23).

The very ones that were supposed to be teaching the truth, (the Son/ Jesus) rejected Him. They didn't know they were rejecting the Son, and that they were also rejecting the Father, who sent the Son. Instead of receiving the "truth," in their wrath they decided to beat Him, and He was beaten with 40 stripes, minus one for you and me (Isaiah 53:5). Yet, the Father could have, but didn't because He knew that Jesus had to go through death for you and me.

I have a question. Would you just watch your only son be beaten with a whip and cut with a knife, with blood pouring out of His body? Just watch, if the Son would not allow you (The Father) to stop them? Can you feel His pain? Can you imagine what He must have gone through and how the Father must have felt? Can you imagine what He was experiencing? Instead of the Father feeling the pain, He was encouraging Jesus to go through the pain and the suffering for you and me. To be the perfect sacrifice without a spot, wrinkle, blemish, or any such thing to let you know that just like Jesus, you can endure all things as long as you have the will of the Father in you.

He was like a sheep, lead to be slaughtered; humble, loving and showing compassion for you and I, (Romans 8:36). But just like a good soldier being obedient, He endured the hardness as unto the Father so that you can endure hardness like a good soldier unto Him (2 Timothy 2:3-5).

Jesus was oppressed and afflicted. Yet, He did not open His mouth (Isaiah 53:7). To be called the devil, be beaten on, to carry His own cross to His death and yet everything that He endured, he did it for you and me. The more that He endured, the closer He was bringing us closer to the Father. Because He was in the world but not of the world, He was doing it for the healing of the nation; to redeem us back to the Father and most of all, to fulfil all of the prophesy that was spoken through the mouths of the Prophets and that He was written in the volume of the book (Hebrews 10:7).

Then, Jesus laid down His life for you and I, but still some people don't want to give Him the glory now. Nor the honor that is due to Him (John10:11). To see us put a crown of thorns on His head, nails in His hands, and we pierce Him in His side, where blood and water came out (John 19:34). The blood was for the atonement (covering) of our sins and the water was for the cleansing of our sin.

Then for three hours, He hung on the cross and finally yelled out, "Eli Eli Lema Sabachthani (my God my God, why have you forsaken me) (Matthews 27:46)."

But God never left Him, nor had he forsaken Him. He had to endure the cross until the very end (Deut. 31:8). No matter what the situation was, He has redeemed us back to our rightful place with our Father. So, all that Jesus did for you, and you tell me that Jesus doesn't deserve the praises, and the honor? That's why God gave Him all the power and authority in heaven and on earth.

At the name of Jesus, every knee shall bow; of those in heaven, of those on and those under the earth. Every tongue shall confess that Jesus is Lord Philippians (2:10:11). Until you realize or understand who Jesus really is in your life, around your life and what He means to you in the bible, you can't really give Him the praise. Do me a favor and take a moment; think about who woke you up this morning, who gave you the breath in your body, the ability to walk and talk. Take another moment and think about how Jesus supplied your needs when you didn't have a way, or see a way. Not only is Jesus our Advocate, He is the Advocate with the Father. If and when we sin, (1 John 2:1) He pleads our cases to the Father (An Advocate is a person who publicity supports or recommends a particular cause or policy).

He (Jesus) is also the Intercessor if and when we pray. Interceding for you to the Father for His will to be done, in and around your life. An intercessor is a person who intervenes on the behalf of another. Especially, in prayer. To intercede is to act or interpose on behalf of someone during difficult times or troublesome times as by pleading or petition. He's interceding with you when you're in trouble. Jesus is a very present help when you're lonely and don't think you have a friend. He is a friend to the friendless. So, you shouldn't praise or worship anyone other than Jesus, not even God.

God has given His son, or redeemer Jesus the power and authority to rule over the earth and also in heaven. Praise means to say or write good things about someone or something; to offer homage in words or in song. Worship means to fall down before (Jesus) or to bow down before (Jesus). You can praise Jesus for the things He has done for you but to really worship Him, you have to worship Him in spirit and in truth.

Just because you speak it, doesn't mean you have the true worship that Jesus is looking for or expecting. When you pray or talk to God, allow God to show, teach, and share with you His worship and praise. No one can tell you how to worship or praise Him. Just like He made everyone individually. He wants you to acknowledge Him on how to celebrate Him coming into your life, to praise Him for all the wonderful things He has done to and for our lives; to worship Him and His precious Holy Ghost.

When you look at this, just think of who's in the middle. God is the Father and the Creator of all things (true). Jesus is the "Word" (John 1:1-7); the Son who God allowed to come on Earth to be not only a Savior to save us from the world, but to establish us in our royal kingdom here on earth. So, when you pray in the Holy Ghost and lift up the name of Jesus, then Jesus gives the glory to God and the Holy Ghost rejoices as well. Then you'll have a perfect flow in the Godheads.

So, the next time you ask God to show you Him, He's going to show you Jesus. The next time you ask God to show you His backside He's going to show you Jesus (Exodus 33:18). So, the next time you ask God to allow you to feel His warmth, His love or His anointing, He is going to show you Jesus. The next time you ask for anything pertaining to His Word, He's going to show you His Word and His Word is Jesus (John 1:1-14). So, the next time you want to lift up God, He's going to give it to Jesus. So, the next time you are praying for peace, The Father is going to point to Jesus who is the Prince of Peace (Isaiah 9:6). So, why are you waiting to give Jesus the praise? Are you waiting for this chapter to be over?

Do you know or understand that Jesus inhabits the praises of His people (Psalms 22:3)?

Inhabits means to live; to dwell in. So, when we praise Jesus, he dwells in them. He gets all over the thanks and the recognition that you give Him. His spirit bonds with yours when you lift His name up. Also, the Bible states, "O give thanks unto the Lord: for He is good: for His mercy endures forever (Psalms 107:1)." Thanks, is another form of giving praises unto the Lord. When you start thanking Jesus for just being God and not asking for anything, not only does God get happy but Jesus starts to smile on your situation and the Holy Ghost starts to move on your behalf. What about entering His gates with thanksgiving and entering His court with praise? Jesus is also instructing you on how to come into the house of God. To enter it with your mind on Jesus and when you come in, thank Him and give Him glory.

What about praise are common for the upright (Psalms 33:1) praise the Lord with the harp? When you're upright with Jesus no one has to tell you to praise/worship Him. It will become automatic. Even when you sing, Praise ye the Lord: for it is good to sing praises unto our God: it is pleasant and praises are comely (Psalms 147:1). It's the will of Christ Jesus pertaining you. The next time, you want to give Jesus a perfect praise, He will come inside of you and direct you how to touch Him in that area.

If you don't praise our Lord and Savior Jesus Christ, God is going to allow the rock to cry out. In other words, God is going to allow the rocks to praise Jesus and the blessing that He had in store for you will not make it to you. "I tell you," he replied. "If they keep quiet, the rocks will cry out," (Luke 19:37-40). So if you're not praising Jesus on Earth how do you think you're going to heaven without praising Him?

"Speak not evil one of another, brethren. He that speaketh evil of his brother, and judgeth his brother, speaketh evil of the law, and judgeth the law: but if thou judge the law, thou art not a doer of the law, but a judge."
James 4: 11

Chapter Eight
It is finished

There is nothing you can pray for or do that's going to be done, that's hasn't already been done, that will be done or that Jesus hasn't defeated on the cross. Jesus isn't going to do anything that's not lined up with His Word and His perfect will.

Too many times we pray, trying to make Jesus do something that He has already done or that's not according to what is written. Did you not know that Jesus stated that He was about His Father's business (Luke 2:49)? That He came to save and set the captives free (Luke 4:18)? So, the Word states that He will perfect (complete) that which concerns me (Psalms 138:8). Until you get into Jesus and His mind frame (1 Corinthians 2:11) and the true purpose and plan for your life, then you won't understand the true purpose of His Word.

If you don't understand the true Word, then you don't know the true Jesus. Then you'll allow everything and anything that comes to upset you because you don't understand His Word nor His plan.

Did you know that while Jesus was on this Earth, He didn't get up with the cares of the World? Did you know that Jesus isn't concerned about Cancer (Breast, liver etc.), aids, sinus, headaches, diabetes or various diseases and sicknesses that are affect and effecting our lives? So that means He's concerned about you getting into the Word so that it (The Word) can manifest in your life so you can be healed. So, He's concerned about the Word manifesting in our lives to defeat the works of the enemy.

So, He has given you a job to do. He has given you the authority through His Word to lay hands on yourself and also to call upon the Elders of the church (James 5:14).

In the Book of Rev. 22:2, there were leaves/fruits for the healing of the nations. Yes, Jesus left leaves and certain fruits as natural healing for the body. If He was concerned about sickness/disease He would never talk about healing in the Word.

Do you know that God isn't concerned about the church? He left a book of instructions called the Bible. If you don't comply with the Word, then God will not allow His presence to move/operate in the church (Ichabod 1 Samuel 4:21). The glory has departed. He gave the church instructions to follow. That means He also gave you a job to do. Jesus asked us to meditate on the Word day and night, so that you can do all that is written in Joshua 1:8. To the leaders, he gave instructions to the ones that are destroying and scattering the sheep of my pasture (Jeremiah 23:1). Also, if you study to show yourself approve unto God (2 Timothy 2:15), then you will not be easily moved/deceived or easily allow the devil to come in.

Do you know that God is not concerned about the government? His Word stated that the government shall be upon His shoulders (Isaiah 9:6). That means he rules and reigns over every government, king and president period. For He is the King of Kings and Lord of Lords.
In Psalms 21:1, He states that the king's heart is in His hands. He guides wherever He pleases. So, that's letting you know that Jesus is over the president, king, queen,

whatever or whoever is in office. But He gave them a commission to pray for those that rule over you (1 Timothy 2:1-3).

God is not concerned about the holidays: Christmas, Easter, etc. Did Jesus state, "don't esteem one day over another (Romans 14:5)?" Also, those are traditions of men and not lined up with His Word. Have you ever read or seen in the Bible where Jesus celebrated Christmas? But yet, that's supposed to be His birthday? But it's not (Luke 1:26). Then the church states that it's a day that we set aside. No, it's not, it's a pagan holiday that we have allowed to enter the church and make a doctrine. Look up Christmas and see what it states. Jeremiah 10 tells us about the Christmas trees and tells us not to be like the pagan (unsaved).

Do you know that God isn't concerned about the weather, wars, and killings (murders)? In the book of Matthews, it is stated that there will be wars and rumors of the Word, but the end is not yet. With the environment, He informed us to speak and it shall come to pass. Did not Joshua speak to the sun and commanded it to stand still until they won the war (Joshua 10:13)? Didn't God allow Moses to not only walk on dry land, but allowed the Red Sea to split (Exodus 14:29)? Did not Jesus and Peter walk on the water? So even the elements are subjects to Jesus. So that wasn't a concern of His. Also, killings: in the book of Rev 6:4, its rider was given power to take peace from the earth and to make people kill each other. Also, with the death (killing, murders) angels: they (children of Israel) put the blood on the doorpost.

So, He's concerned about you being covered with the blood (Exodus 12:13). The blood on the doorposts will be a sign to mark the houses in which you live. So, instead of praying for no more killing, because the hardness or corruption of people's hearts and minds they will be killing, pray that the people get/ be covered with the blood (Jesus Word) until they make a right decision to accept Jesus Christ as their personal Savior. Once they do that, they'll grow in grace (study, go to church read the Word) and in the knowledge of the Son of Man (2 Peter 3:18).

Also, about the music worshiping and praising Him, Jesus doesn't accept everything. Just because you love it, doesn't mean He likes it! The Bible states that when we sing up to Him, that the song be Holy (not rap, jazz, old school, or country reggae). Psalms 96:1; sing a new song isn't the things that's mentioned above is old music? Ephesians 5:19; spiritual songs, the above aren't spiritual. You can't come to God with the junk we call music and expect God's anointing to be upon. Psalms 150; "Praise ye the Lord, Praise Him in the Sanctuary," so how can you really give Him praise and you're not saved? You really don't know Him if you're not saved. You can go through the motions and even have a feeling but if you're not saved, you don't know him. True, He died for you, but you are not His.

So, it's time that the Real Church of God, stand up and be about our father's business, line ourselves up with the Word and not the cares of this world.

Jesus understand that at times we are going to get weak and have concern, but He also left us a Word for that as well. He tells us to cast our cares upon Him because He cares for us (Psalms 55:22, 1 Peter 5:7). And while you're on the battle fields, going to the highway and hedges, (Luke 14:23) compelling people to come to church and your laboring is getting hard. The Word states that all those who Labor and have heavy laden. He (Jesus) stated, come upon Him and He shall give you rest. So, if you still want to pray and expect Jesus to perform a miracle that's not lined up with his Word, I'm going to have to ask you to make sure that what you're praying for is in His Word and look to see if it's according to His will.

In Matthews 6, Jesus left us a model prayer that we be about our father's business. Look at verse number 10, "Your kingdom come, Your will be done, not our will." So, while reading these sentences, paragraphs and various statements, it goes back to the first couple of statements: there is nothing you can pray for or do that's going to be done, that's hasn't already been done, that will be done or that Jesus hasn't defeated on the cross.

The last thing that Jesus defeated was death; "O' death where is your sting and grave where's your victory (1 Corinthians 15:55)."

It is finished

"So, Joshua conquered all the land: the mountain country and the South and the lowland and the wilderness slopes, and all their kings; he left none remaining, but utterly destroyed all that breathed, as the Lord God of Israel had commanded."

Joshua 10:40

Meet the Author

John Mask is originally from Gary, Indiana. The eight of ten children, and the youngest of three boys. His parents, Floyd Mask Sr. and Darlene Nelson, divorced when he was a child. His father was a steel worker and mother worked as a delivery room technician. His mother had a tough time raising the ten children by herself but made the best of the situation by ensuring the and his siblings were constantly in church. As a teenager, John played junior high and high school sports at Bailey Junior High and Lee Wallace High School, both in Gary, Indiana. As a young man without strict oversight and guidance he spent a period of his life experiencing the street-life and hanging out with gangs. This lifestyle nearly consumed him, but the Lord had a way of turning him around when his family relocated to Brownsville, Tennessee. John now has three beautiful children, Marquita, Joshua, and Ashante. He spends most of this time preaching the gospel and writing poetry, and now resides in Memphis, Tennessee.

"I can do all things through Christ who strengthens me"

Philippians 4:13

"But those who wait on the Lord shall renew their strength, they shall mount up with wings like eagles, they shall run and not be weary, they shall walk and not faint."

Isaiah 40:31

Got an idea for a book? Contact Curry Brothers Books, LLC. We are not satisfied until your publishing dreams come true. We specialize in all genres of books, especially religion, leadership, family history, poetry, and children's literature. There is an African Proverb that confirms, "When an elder dies a library closes." Be careful who tells your family history. Are their values your family's values? Our staff will navigate you through the entire publishing process and take pride in going the extra mile by exceeding your publishing goals.

Improving the world one book at a time!

Curry Brothers Books, LLC PO Box 247
Haymarket, VA 20168
(719) 466-7518 & (615) 347-9124
Visit us at www.currybrothersbooks.com

CURRY BROS.
MARKETING + PUBLISHING GROUP

CPSIA information can be obtained
at www.ICGtesting.com
Printed in the USA
JSHW050825181020
8823JS00001B/1